Visual Geography Series®

IRELAND

...in Pictures

Prepared by
Geography Department

Lerner Publications Company
Minneapolis

Independent Picture Service

In western Ireland, a young girl pets her family's donkey.

This book is an all-new edition of the Visual Geography Series. Previous editions were published by Sterling Publishing Company, New York City. The text, set in 10/12 Century Textbook, is fully revised and updated, and new photographs, maps, charts, and captions have been added.

LIBRARY OF CONGRESS CATALOGING-IN-PUBLICATION DATA

Ireland in pictures / prepared by Geography Department, Lerner Publications Company.
  p.˙ cm. – (Visual geography series)
  Rev. ed. of: Ireland in pictures / prepared by Rhoda Fagen and others.
  Includes bibliographical references.
  Summary: Introduces the geography, history, government, people, economy, and culture of the "Emerald Isle."
  ISBN 0-8225-1878-3
  1. Ireland – Juvenile literature. [1. Ireland.] I. Fagen, Rhoda. Ireland in pictures. II. Lerner Publications Company. Geography Dept. III. Series: Visual geography series (Minneapolis, Minn.)
DA906.I74 1990
941.5 – dc20   90–34973

International Standard Book Number: 0-8225-1878-3
Library of Congress Card Catalog Number: 90-34973

VISUAL GEOGRAPHY SERIES®

Publisher
Harry Jonas Lerner
Associate Publisher
Nancy M. Campbell
Senior Editor
Mary M. Rodgers
Editors
Gretchen Bratvold
Dan Filbin
Phyllis Schuster
Photo Researcher
Kerstin Coyle
Editorial/Photo Assistants
Marybeth Campbell
Consultants/Contributors
Christabel D. Grant
Sandra K. Davis
Designer
Jim Simondet
Cartographer
Carol F. Barrett
Indexers
Kristine I. Spangard
Sylvia Timian
Production Manager
Gary J. Hansen

Independent Picture Service

Probably dating from the sixth century, this Irish tombstone is marked with a Christian cross and an early form of writing.

Acknowledgments

Title page photo by Irish Tourist Board, Dublin.

Elevation contours adapted from *The Times Atlas of the World*, seventh comprehensive edition (New York: Times Books, 1985).

A couple walk along a narrow country lane on one of the Aran Islands. A network of walled fields crisscrosses these islands, which lie off Ireland's western coast. Made from the stones that were cleared from the land, the walls keep farm animals within specific grazing areas.

Contents

IRELAND

N ↑

--- County Boundaries

—— Major Roads

0   25   50 Miles

0   25   50 Kilometers

SCOTLAND

NORTHERN IRELAND

Donegal
Town

Armagh

IRISH SEA

*Lough
Conn*

Moy R.

*Lough
Allen*

Clew Bay

Louisburgh

*Lough
Mask*

Cong

*Lough
Corrib*

*Lough
Ree*

Royal Canal

NEWGRANGE
(Ruins)

Boyne R.

MEATH
Maynooth

Holyhead

Galway

Grand Canal

KILDARE

DUBLIN

Dublin Bay

ATLANTIC

ARAN
ISLANDS

Killimer

Shannon R.

*Lough
Derg*

Glendalough

Nore R.

Barrow R.

OCEAN

Shannon

Limerick

Kilkenny

Tarbert

Ardagh

Tipperary

Suir R.

Waterford

Rosslare

Dingle

Killarney

*L.
Leane*

*Lakes of
Killarney*

Lee R.

*Caragh
R.*

Cork

Kinsale

WALES

Pembroke

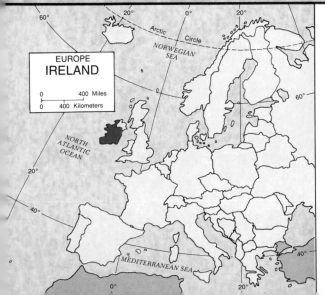

60°

20°

0°

20°

Arctic Circle

*NORWEGIAN
SEA*

60°

EUROPE
IRELAND

0   400 Miles

0   400 Kilometers

*NORTH
ATLANTIC
OCEAN*

20°

20°

40°

40°

MEDITERRANEAN SEA

0°

20°

METRIC CONVERSION CHART
To Find Approximate Equivalents

WHEN YOU KNOW:	MULTIPLY BY:	TO FIND:
AREA		
acres	0.41	hectares
square miles	2.59	square kilometers
CAPACITY		
gallons	3.79	liters
LENGTH		
feet	30.48	centimeters
yards	0.91	meters
miles	1.61	kilometers
MASS (weight)		
pounds	0.45	kilograms
tons	0.91	metric tons
VOLUME		
cubic yards	0.77	cubic meters
TEMPERATURE		
degrees Fahrenheit	0.56 (*after* subtracting 32)	degrees Celsius

Ireland's rocky landscape is a playground for these children, who live near a seaside resort in western Ireland.

Introduction

The Republic of Ireland—called *Eire* in Gaelic, one of the country's official languages—is an independent nation that occupies most of the island of Ireland. Lying in the Atlantic Ocean at the western edge of Europe, Ireland has been invaded several times during the last 2,000 years. At various periods, different ethnic groups crossed the sea from Great Britain to the east and from the continent of Europe to the south. The most recent conquerors came from Great Britain.

In 1921, after hundreds of years of unbroken foreign rule, all but six counties in the island's northeastern corner achieved self-government. Political leaders in northeastern Ireland decided to maintain ties with Great Britain. That area of the island is now known as Northern Ireland.

Ireland's moist, mild climate is one of the country's main features. Lush grasslands that are watered by frequent rains make Ireland a farming nation. But the wet climate also limits farming to crops that

5

During the potato famine of the 1840s, farm families worked hard to scratch a living from the land. Many Irish people died from hunger and disease because a fungus spoiled the potato crops—the staple food for Ireland's rural population.

can grow in poorly drained soil. More than half of Ireland's inhabitants are urban dwellers, but most of them live in small cities and towns that maintain ties with the countryside. Livestock raising—a principal part of the nation's economy—supports a way of life that has been basically rural for centuries.

In the 1840s, a succession of poor harvests due to diseased crops made it impossible for farmers to earn their living. A fungus destroyed the potato crop, leaving many people hungry and causing thousands to die. As a result, large numbers of Irish people emigrated from their homeland. Even after the potato famine had ended, however, people continued to leave Ireland. They sought better economic opportunities in Great Britain, the United States, Canada, and Australia. Not until the 1960s did the large number of people leaving Ireland begin to decrease.

The loss of so many people during the early twentieth century had a negative effect on Ireland's economy. Fewer people farmed the land successfully, and businesses frequently failed. Since the 1960s, Ireland's birthrate has been among the highest in Europe. This rapidly growing population was one factor that led to an unemployment rate of roughly 20 percent. Improving the economy is Ireland's principal challenge of the 1990s.

A member of the European Community since 1973, Ireland has broadened trade with much of Europe. Cooperation with other nations has improved the country's potential for economic recovery. Through these measures—as well as through growth opportunities at home—the Irish government hopes to give its citizens reasons to invest in Ireland's future.

Ireland's history has included the arrival of many foreigners. They constructed buildings, such as this abbey, throughout the country. The abbey is now a boarding school run by Roman Catholic nuns.

Courtesy of Richard Rodgers

Photo by Christabel D. Grant

A busy street in Galway City reflects Ireland's economic progress. On this summer day, the city celebrates the opening of its new radio station.

Rugged mountains dwarf Bally-nahinch Castle, which overlooks blue lakes and fast-flowing rivers. Now a resort, the castle offers visitors a base from which to explore western Ireland.

Photo by Irish Tourist Board, Dublin

1) The Land

Ireland is the second largest island in the British Isles, a group of landmasses that also includes Great Britain. Occupying five-sixths of the island of Ireland, the Republic of Ireland covers 27,136 square miles—an area about the size of the state of South Carolina.

The remaining one-sixth forms Northern Ireland, which is part of the United Kingdom of Great Britain and Northern Ireland. About 50 miles to the east—across the Irish Sea—lie Wales, Scotland, and England, which are also part of the United Kingdom. The Atlantic Ocean surrounds Ireland on the north, west, and south.

Topography

Lush vegetation covers Ireland, especially along the seacoast and in the country's

Sheep graze in the rolling green countryside that is typical of Ireland's central plain.

many rolling valleys. A fertile central plain and mountain ranges that surround the plain compose Ireland's two topographic regions.

The central plain is used as farmland, mostly as pasture for livestock. The soil has a limestone base and includes deposits of sand and clay. Peat bogs—former swamps that contain partially decayed vegetation—cover about 8 percent of the country.

In places where the Shannon River flows, the central plain is extremely fertile. In the low mountains that encircle the plain, the land is generally barren. The interior is marked by many twisting rivers. Some of the waterways spill into the sea, while others broaden into deep lakes.

The rocky, windswept mountains along Ireland's western coast jut into the sea. Steep cliffs also rise above small islands —most notably the Aran Islands—in this area. The sea has carved bays between the coastal mountains. These long inlets reach into Ireland so deeply that no location on the island is more than 70 miles from the

The Caragh River curves through southwestern Ireland to the Atlantic Ocean. Small streams crisscross the nation, providing opportunities for fishing as well as sightseeing.

sea. Filling out the circle in the west are the Nephin Mountains, and in the northwest are the Blue Stack and Derryveagh mountains.

Like the western coast, Ireland's eastern coast is studded with mountains, including the Wicklow range. In the south, running east to west, are several other chains—the Comeragh, the Knockmealdown, and the Galty mountains. Ireland's highest peak is Carrantuohill (3,414 feet) in Macgillycuddy Reeks, a range in the southwestern part of the island.

Rivers and Lakes

Beginning in northwestern Ireland and flowing through mountains and plains, the

Photo by Edward Smith

Croagh Patrick rises in northwestern Ireland near Clew Bay. Traditionally associated with Saint Patrick—the missionary who brought Christianity to Ireland—the mountain is treeless, steep, and rocky. Pilgrims travel to the site each year, climbing part of the way without shoes.

Independent Picture Service

Reaching more than 600 feet above sea level, the Cliffs of Moher stretch five miles along Ireland's southern coast. The nineteenth-century tower that sits at the top was built for viewing the countryside rather than for military defense.

Boats can navigate the Shannon River—Ireland's longest and most important waterway—for more than half of its 230-mile course. Eventually, the river broadens into several lakes that average 25 miles long and 3 miles wide.

Located in eastern Ireland amid the Wicklow Mountains, Glendalough actually consists of two lakes. In this region also lie some of Ireland's most famous religious ruins, many of which date from the sixth century.

Shannon River is the longest river in the British Isles. Extending over 230 miles, the waterway travels through a series of lakes (*loughs* in Gaelic)—Lough Allen, Lough Ree, and Lough Dearg. The river then empties into the Atlantic Ocean on Ireland's western coast. The mouth of the Shannon forms a long bay that serves the port of Limerick.

The Liffey River starts in the Wicklow Mountains and flows in a northeasterly direction. It cuts through Dublin—the capital of the republic—and empties into the Irish Sea at Dublin Bay. Other small rivers water the island, contributing to the deep-green hillsides and valleys. The Nore, Suir, Lee, and Barrow rivers run through southeastern Ireland. The Boyne courses through the northeast, and the Moy flows in the northwest.

The Irish use many short rivers for transportation and for fishing. Some waterways feed local bodies of water, for example the Lakes of Killarney—Lower Lake, Muckcross Lake, and Upper Lake—in the southwest.

Climate

Ireland has a wet and mild climate. Temperatures in summer average around 60° F, and winter temperatures hover near 40° F. Incoming winds and the interior's nearness to the sea help to make Ireland's summers cool and its winters mild. Most of the time the wind blows from the southwest, passing over the waters of the Gulf Stream current in the Atlantic Ocean. In summer, the ocean cools the winds that blow across the island, bringing colder temperatures. In winter, the sea warms the winds passing over it, which consequently raises the temperature on the island.

These winds also carry plentiful rainfall to all parts of Ireland. The frequent rains

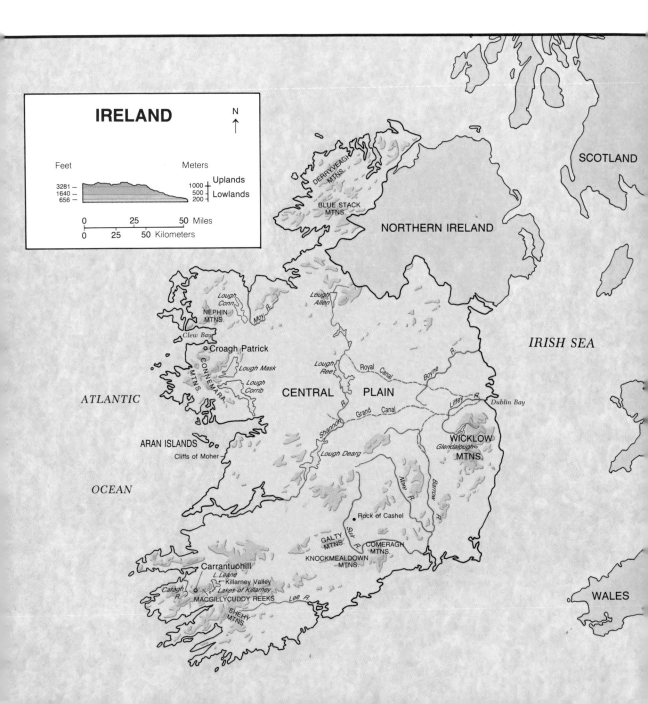

Taking cover during a sudden storm, a young Irish boy crouches beneath a rock. The Irish are accustomed to the island's frequent rainfalls, which occur throughout the year.

The Lakes of Killarney glisten beneath the mountains of Macgillycuddy Reeks in southwestern Ireland. Of different sizes and shapes, the lakes are part of a scenic area that includes dense vegetation.

Although Ireland is noted for its year-round greenery, autumn brings flaming colors to some of the nation's trees.

13

Artwork by Laura Westlund

The shamrock, a three-leafed plant of the clover family, is Ireland's national emblem. According to tradition, Saint Patrick used the shamrock to talk about the Holy Trinity (the three-part concept of the Christian God).

make the country's soil highly productive, especially in the river valleys. Some of the flat lands, however, have become bogs— marshy areas created by heavy rainfall and inadequate soil drainage. These two factors cause the surface vegetation to decay. Layers of partly decayed vegetation build up into a spongy material called peat, or turf. Peat may be cut, dried, and used as fuel. Bogs cleared of peat sometimes are planted with trees.

Flora and Fauna

A land bridge once linked Ireland to Europe, but the connection disappeared about 7,000 years ago. As a result, the variety of animals and plants found in Ireland is much smaller than in other parts of Europe. In addition, human settlement and farming patterns have destroyed the habitats of many plants and animals that are still found on the island. Nevertheless, a thick growth of lush vegetation has given Ireland the nickname the Emerald Isle. (Emerald is a vivid shade of green.)

Photo by Irish Tourist Board, Dublin

Offering oats as a reward, a horse trainer schools some Connemara ponies in western Ireland. These animals are the only breed of horses native to the country. Sometimes found in the wild, Connemara ponies are gentle enough for young riders.

14

Photo by Irish Tourist Board, Dublin

Hikers, as well as people traveling by car, enjoy the scenery in the pine forests of the Shehy Mountains.

Courtesy of Irish Tourist Board, New York

South of Dublin, a field of purple heather and yellow gorse stands below one of the region's rounded mountaintops.

The southwestern part of Ireland has the island's most varied plant life. Rhododendrons and fuchsia bushes grow wild in peat bogs. Many kinds of ferns and rushes (hollow-stemmed plants) cover the marshy areas of Ireland.

In some parts of the republic, there are thick stands of oak, birch, ash, hazel, alder, and willow trees. Governmental efforts have increased Ireland's forested regions from 1 percent to 5 percent of the total land area. One of the island's densest original forests, Killarney Valley, is rich with ferns and mosses.

The remains of now-extinct animals—such as the giant Irish deer, arctic foxes, and arctic lemmings (rodents that turned white in winter)—have been unearthed in caves. Some of these bones are 40,000 years old. In the present era, very few kinds of land mammals survive in Ireland. A breed of horse known as Connemara ponies are native to Ireland and are often used to carry inexperienced riders. Foxes, badgers, otters, and Irish hares are abundant, and freshwater sponges (aquatic animals) inhabit Ireland's lakes. Made of interconnected fibers that form the animals' skeletons, Ireland's sponge species exist nowhere else in Europe.

Cities

An average of 133 people live in each square mile of Ireland. More than half of the Irish make their homes in cities and

16

medium-sized towns. With about 916,000 people, Dublin is Ireland's largest city and its capital. It is also the manufacturing, business, and cultural hub of the nation. The Liffey River, which empties into the Irish Sea, divides the city in half. The Grand and Royal canals were built in the 1800s to connect the capital to the Shannon River. The canals once were used to transport goods to Dublin, but in modern times tourists use the waterways for sightseeing.

Dublin's main streets are wide, and the city has many public squares and parks—including Phoenix Park and the Botanical Gardens. Conquerors of Ireland built a number of the capital's landmark buildings hundreds of years ago. Vikings from Denmark first constructed Christ Church Cathedral in the eleventh century, and Normans—invaders whose ancestors came to England from France—sponsored the building of St. Patrick's Cathedral in the twelfth century. In the thirteenth century, the Normans founded Dublin Castle, which later became the center of British authority in Ireland.

Dublin is the site of the University of Dublin, known as Trinity College. Also in Dublin are Leinster House, the gathering

O'Connell Street, a wide thoroughfare in downtown Dublin, accommodates many cars, pedestrians, and memorial statues.

Photo by Irish Tourist Board, Dublin

17

place for the national legislature, and the Four Courts, the seat of the nation's judiciary.

Cork (population 174,000) is the second largest city in Ireland. Located on the island's southern coast, Cork has a harbor that can handle a large number of ships. The city is also an important shipbuilding center. Limerick (population 75,000), on the western coast of Ireland, is an agricultural and industrial hub for the region. In addition to its economic activities, this city hosts a drama and dance festival every March.

Many smaller Irish towns—Galway, Waterford, Killarney, Tipperary, and Kilkenny, for example—are known for regional industries that include brewing beer and ale, manufacturing glass, and making cheese. These towns are also market centers for farm families and draw many tourists to Ireland.

On its way eastward to the Irish Sea, the Liffey River cuts through Dublin, the capital of the Republic of Ireland. The river divides the city into northern and southern halves. Bridges and embankments offer pleasant walkways for the capital's residents, who are called Dubliners.

Photo by Michelle Hannah

Trinity College is one of Dublin's most famous landmarks. Although the university was founded in 1591, none of the original buildings still exist. Laws reserved enrollment at the university for male Protestants until 1793, when male Roman Catholics were also allowed to attend. Women were first admitted to Trinity in 1903. The college houses one of the largest libraries in the world and includes rare, hand-painted manuscripts, such as the ninth-century Book of Kells.

Tourists and residents of Ireland enjoy the nation's beaches, especially on sunny days when swimming and sunbathing are comfortable.

Courtesy of Tim Weinhold

Christianity has been central to the development of Irish culture and history since the fifth century. Christian monks created the Book of Kells, a beautiful copy of the Christian Gospels. It features an art form known as illumination—ornate hand-writing and finely drawn illustrations that are flecked with bright colors and real gold.

Courtesy of Minneapolis Public Library and Information Center

2) History and Government

Archaeologists think that humans were living in Ireland by about 3000 B.C. Tombs of these first Irish were built in several distinctive designs. Most were made of stone, and some had open gathering areas next to the burial chambers. Some people were buried in earthen mounds built on hill-tops. Inside of the tombs, mourners placed objects that were treasured by the first Irish. These items included jewelry, pot-tery, weapons, and utensils made from animal bones.

Called beaker pottery, the ceramic works from these burial sites are similar in style to items made in Great Britain and on the continent of Europe. The original inhabitants of Ireland hunted game and snared fish to survive. But most of the early Irish had turned to farming by 2000 B.C. They also became good metalworkers, making objects of gold, copper, and bronze. Examples of Irish metalwork have been discovered on mainland Europe, suggesting that trade occurred between the two regions.

The Celts Arrive

By 250 B.C., groups of Celtic people had arrived in Ireland. Originally from northeastern Europe, the Celts spread to France, Spain, Greece, and the British Isles. They were a warlike people who made their weapons from iron. They used an artistic style that featured curves and spirals to decorate their tombs and dwellings. Although their influence in Europe was brief, the Celts remained strong in the British Isles. In England, Wales, Scotland, and Ireland, they maintained their identity by spreading their language, arts, and customs throughout the region.

The Irish Celts had many leaders, each of whom controlled a small kingdom called a *tuatha*. A tuatha was composed of people descended from a common ancestor, and its ruler—called a chief—was elected from the tuatha's upper class. The Celts also had poets, legal advisers (called *brehon*), priests (called Druids), and common people in their communities. Only occasionally did one tuatha combine with another for defense or for some other mutual benefit. Most Celtic groups were fiercely independent.

The residents of Ireland called their homeland *Eriu* (Erin) and named themselves *Goidil* (Gael). The Druids, scholarly priests who claimed to have divine knowledge, strongly influenced Celtic society.

In ancient times, perhaps as early as 3000 B.C., Irish people built monuments made of large stones. Two upright rocks were covered by a third stone, which served as a roof. Known as megaliths, these structures were probably used as tombs.

Photo by Edward Smith

A large rock, called a kerbstone, lies in front of this tomb entrance and is covered with the swirling, circular art of the early Celtic people. Located at Newgrange in County Meath, this long burial chamber was precisely constructed so that sunshine entered it at specific times of the year.

Photo by Christabel D. Grant

These priests advised the chiefs on most community matters and on important political questions.

Beginning in the fourth century, several chiefs gained control of a number of tuatha and thereby enlarged their kingdoms. The division of Ireland into five major territories—called the five-fifths—developed when chiefs governed these areas for long periods of time. Ulster, Connacht, Munster, Leinster, and Meath became the five political units of Ireland.

With more than 100 tuatha fighting among themselves, it was difficult for a single chief, or king, to control the entire island. Niall of the Nine Hostages, who reigned from A.D. 380 to 405, was the first chief to rule nearly all of Ireland. Niall gained his name after conquering other tuatha and taking nine important hostages.

Saint Patrick and Christian Ireland

Niall and other chiefs made many conquests on the island of Great Britain and on mainland Europe as well. Among the captives was an upper-class 16-year-old boy who may have come from what is now Wales. He would later be known as Saint Patrick. Sold as a slave in about A.D. 405, Patrick herded animals in northeastern Ireland for several years. He escaped to Europe in 411 and eventually became a Christian priest and missionary.

In 432 Patrick returned to Ireland as a missionary and converted many of the Irish to Christianity. The center of his activity was northeastern Ireland, where he and other missionaries taught the Latin language to many of their converts. Monasteries (religious communities of men or women) developed in Ireland during Patrick's era, becoming centers of worship in the tuatha. The monasteries also established schools that attracted students from many parts of Europe.

Beginning in the sixth century, some monks went to Great Britain and to mainland Europe as missionaries. The monasteries and their schools became centers of learning, teaching many academic subjects —such as Latin, geometry, and astronomy—as well as religion.

During the sixth century, the work of the monks and their schools fostered the beginnings of Gaelic literature, music, and local arts. One of the era's most beautiful arts was calligraphy (ornate hand-lettering). Monks copied religious texts and

The Ardagh Chalice is an example of early Irish-Christian art. Fashioned in the eighth century of silver, gold, and brass, the chalice was discovered in the 1800s in a potato field near the town of Ardagh in County Limerick.

This granite statue of Saint Patrick commemorates the 1500th anniversary of the missionary's landing in Ireland. "Saint Patrick" is written in the Gaelic language at the base of the memorial.

decorated them with intricate designs and vibrant colors. The most famous manuscript done in this fashion is the Book of Kells, a copy of the Christian Gospels made in about the eighth century.

Viking Invasions

At the end of the eighth century, sea raiders from Norway and Denmark invaded Ireland. Called Vikings, these raiders sailed up Ireland's rivers to reach far into the interior. They attacked monasteries, killed many monks, and took precious religious objects as their treasure. In time, some of the invaders began to settle and trade in the region, founding the cities now known as Dublin, Cork, Limerick, and Waterford.

By the mid-ninth century, Irish chiefs began to successfully resist the Vikings who continued to raid the island. Viking defeats allowed the tuatha to unify for defense. By the eleventh century, they had combined under Brian Boru, who became the king of Ireland. Brian Boru's fighters decisively defeated the Vikings near Dublin at the Battle of Clontarf in 1014. Although the Irish were successful, Brian Boru was killed during the battle, and the Irish again splintered into separate tuatha.

Some Vikings fled home by sea, but many remained in Ireland and were absorbed over time into the Irish population. The Viking invasions had a significant impact on Irish life. With the development of Viking trading communities, the centers of population gradually shifted from inland areas to newer coastal settlements.

Some of the Irish, however, remained in rural regions during this war-torn era. In these areas, native and Viking architectural styles were combined in the design of many stone churches. Near their churches, monks built towers that served as lookout posts and places of refuge.

The Normans Come to Ireland

For about 150 years, the Irish farmed their land in peace. They were invaded again, however, this time by the Normans, who were originally from Normandy in France. Skilled fighters, the Normans had conquered England in 1066 and had taken over the English throne. By the early 1100s, they turned their attention to Ireland.

Using metal armor, crossbows, and longbows, the Normans attacked the Irish forces. The Irish chiefs, who had fallen into disunity after the death of Brian Boru, were not able to combine their troops to fight the Norman soldiers. The separate

Photo by Irish Tourist Board, Dublin

In the ninth century, Viking raiders from Norway and Denmark invaded Ireland in wooden warships. Designed to sail swiftly up rivers, these boats allowed the Vikings to surprise and harass the Irish Celts.

Courtesy of Irish Tourist Board, New York

Standing upon a huge limestone base, a walled town called the Rock of Cashel was a defensive site as well as a religious center for the Irish king of Munster. Inhabited before the time of Saint Patrick, the locale has held many castle and cathedral buildings throughout the centuries.

Irish armies resisted fiercely, but their axes and swords were a poor match for the iron weapons and superior training of their opponents.

By the mid-1200s, the Normans had established walled towns in many parts of Ireland. Irish chiefs in the north and west still maintained their independence. The Norman kings of England introduced feudalism to Ireland—a system of land-ownership and authority. Under feudalism, the king owned all the land, and he granted use of it to nobles who promised loyalty, service, and money in return. The nobles made similar arrangements with farmers who actually worked the land.

The Norman kings also introduced their legal code and style of governing to Ireland. The territory was divided into counties, and the Norman leaders set up a local council and civil administrators. By the end of the thirteenth century, a parliament began meeting to set taxes and to make laws. At this same time in England, the distinction between Normans and English began to blur as intermarriage produced a Norman-English population.

Occasionally, the Irish chiefs tried to regain their power. In 1270, for example, the chief of Connacht defeated a Norman-English force. Warriors from Scotland joined the Irish. Norman nobles who were

Walled cities were fully equipped to handle the needs of daily living. This blacksmith's shop sits just inside the walls of one Irish town.

Photo by Michelle Hannah

longtime residents of Ireland also aided the Irish because they hoped to free themselves from the restrictions imposed by the Norman-English kings.

As the Irish armies grew stronger, the Norman-English kings tried to lessen the Irish threat by making new laws. They made it a crime for the Irish to speak Gaelic (their own language) or to buy weapons. The Normans and the longtime English settlers in Ireland were forbidden to have Irish musicians in their homes, to dress in an Irish fashion, or to use the Irish language.

Despite these strict measures, the Irish chiefs and their Norman allies continued to fight the Norman English for control of Ireland in the 1300s and 1400s. The area of English authority—known as the Pale—was reduced to territory in eastern Ireland centered around Dublin. The Irish outside the Pale began using the Celtic law

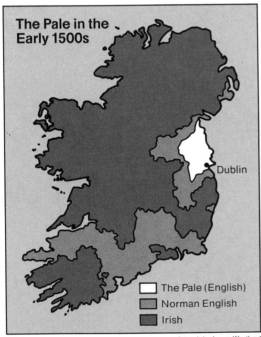

The Pale in the Early 1500s

Dublin

☐ The Pale (English)
▨ Norman English
■ Irish

Artwork by Laura Westlund

In the 1300s and 1400s, the territory of the Pale—the area of English control in Ireland—centered around Dublin. The borders of the Pale expanded and contracted with the arrival and departure of English troops and immigrants.

code of the ancient brehon rather than English law to govern themselves.

In the late 1400s, one of the most powerful English nobles in Ireland—Gerald Fitzgerald, the Earl of Kildare—challenged the rights of the English king Henry VII. Henry sought to bring Ireland under his direct control. He wanted to rid the island of traditions that bolstered Irish identity and to limit local power. Henry sent Edward Poynings to Ireland to act in the king's name. With his authority, Poynings allowed the Irish Parliament to pass only those laws that Henry VII approved—an action with which the earl strongly disagreed. To prevent civil war, Poynings captured Fitzgerald. Soon afterward, however, Poynings lost the support of the king, who released Fitzgerald.

The Irish and the Reformation

A renewed attack on Ireland's independence came after Henry VII's son, Henry VIII, became the king of England. In the late 1530s, Henry VIII tried to impose a new religion—Protestantism—on Ireland. Under the Protestant faith, the king would replace the pope as head of the church, and Ireland's centuries-old ties with Roman Catholicism would end.

In 1541—in an effort to gain political and religious support—Henry took the title of king of Ireland. He offered more land to Irish nobles, but most of them maintained their traditional positions and refused to recognize the English king as head of the church.

During the course of the attempted religious reformation in Ireland, churches were looted and many monasteries were destroyed. The king made it illegal for Roman Catholic monasteries to exist in Ireland. Beyond the area of English authority, however, Catholic religious groups continued to function, despite having fewer resources and less freedom.

During Henry VIII's reign, only a small number of Irish became Protestants. Un-

In the 1530s, the English king Henry VIII named himself head of the new Protestant religion in England. The Irish, who were mainly Roman Catholic, remained faithful to the Roman Catholic Church. In 1541 the English Parliament proclaimed Henry VIII king of Ireland. He tried to get Irish nobles to accept Protestantism by offering them land and titles of nobility. Few Irish became Protestants during Henry's reign.

der his son Edward VI—who ruled from 1547 to 1553—the English government made laws establishing Protestantism as the official religion in Ireland. The English seized the land of many Irish chiefs and their followers who protested this change. Edward awarded their holdings to English Protestants. This transfer of Irish territory to English ownership was known as the plantation system, because English people were artificially "planted" on Irish soil. Edward's successors—Mary I and later Elizabeth I—continued these transfers of land.

IRELAND UNDER ELIZABETH I

Elizabeth I became ruler of England in 1558. The Irish Parliament—which was under English control—named Elizabeth head of the Irish church in 1560. English, rather than Gaelic, became the language used in religious services. The Irish people resented the imposition of the Protes-tant religion, the takeover of their lands, and the second prohibition of the use of their language within 300 years.

Hugh O'Neill of Tyrone—an Irish leader from the province of Ulster—attacked Elizabeth's English troops in 1594 and defeated them at Armagh. Other Irish chiefs fought against the English, and soon the plantations of Munster province were wiped out. To put down the Irish rebellion, a large English force arrived in Ireland in 1599. O'Neill asked Spain—England's rival—for help. When the small Spanish fleet came to Ireland, its commander insisted on mounting a surprise attack. The English defeated the Irish and Spanish forces at the Battle of Kinsale in 1601.

To prevent other revolts from breaking out in Ireland, the English removed all Irish legal and religious rights and resumed the plantation system. The Irish became increasingly resentful of England's presence in Ireland.

Photo by Irish Tourist Board, Dublin

Dublin Castle has gone through several architectural phases in its long history. In its present form, the castle has an eighteenth-century style, although some of its towers *(here hidden from view)* date from the 1400s.

Irish Rebellions Continue

In the 1600s, Irish opposition to English rule frequently resulted in clashes. In 1641 a group of rebels attacked Dublin Castle, the headquarters of the English administration. Although they did not capture the castle, Irish fighters forced many English settlers from their plantations. In 1642 Irish Catholics established a government that rivaled the English monarch's authority. Although troops from England tried to crush the Irish independence movement, they were not successful for several years.

In 1649, however, soldier-politician Oliver Cromwell landed in Dublin with 20,000 English troops. In 1652, in an attack known as "Cromwell's Curse," his army killed many of the people in Dublin and defeated the main body of the Irish forces. Under Cromwell's authority, the English seized more Irish land.

Courtesy of James H. Marrinan

An Irish coin *(top)* carries a likeness of James II, the English king who tried to reestablish good relations with Ireland. His son-in-law and daughter, William and Mary *(bottom)* overthrew James in 1690 and enacted laws that punished the Irish for their religious beliefs.

28

The English kings Charles II (1660–1685) and James II (1685–1690) tried to reestablish good relations with Ireland by restoring some rights to the Irish. These changes were reversed, however, when the Protestant prince William challenged the right of James II—a Roman Catholic—to rule England and Ireland. In 1690 William's forces defeated James's troops at a battle near the Boyne River, and William III became king of England and Ireland. The Irish Parliament—which was Protestant at this time—passed laws that punished Catholics for their religious beliefs. Catholics could not buy land or engage in trade. The laws limited professional and educational opportunities for Irish Catholics and denied them the right to vote.

In the early 1700s, Irish Catholics—who made up most of the population—held only about 10 percent of the land in Ireland. At the same time, England, Wales, and Scotland combined to form the United Kingdom of Great Britain (called Britain or the UK). Jonathan Swift—an Irish writer—chronicled the difficulties of the Irish in bitter articles and satiric stories. His words brought many of the injustices in Ireland to the attention of English people for the first time. Reforms, however, were slow in coming.

A Protestant clergyman and author, Jonathan Swift wrote pamphlets and books that strongly urged the British to treat the Irish fairly. Through his friends in the British government, Swift was able to educate politicians about injustices in Ireland. In recognition of his political work, Queen Anne named Swift head of St. Patrick's Cathedral in Dublin, Swift's birthplace.

PROTESTANT IRELAND

In the eighteenth century, about one-tenth of the Irish population were members of the Church of Ireland—a branch of the Protestant Church of England. This minority of Irish controlled the politics and economy of the entire island for much of the century, during a period called the Protestant Ascendancy. Many Irish Catholic soldiers and politicians fled their country for mainland Europe, where they could achieve success and advancement in foreign armies.

In the 1770s, while Britain was fighting in the American Revolutionary War to keep its North American colonies, Irish Protestants saw an opportunity to gain their independence. Since the British army was busy in North America, few British soldiers were left in Ireland. Irish Protestants established an army called the Irish Volunteers to protect the island from attack by France or Spain, who had declared war on the UK. Many Irish-Protestant business leaders wanted economic as well as political freedom from Britain. The leaders of the volunteers bought their military supplies from Irish merchants rather than from British sources.

Losing ground in North America, the British government found the force of 40,000 volunteers in Ireland too powerful to ignore. Britain gave in to the Protestants' request for a more independent parliament, which gained some authority to make laws. In 1783 Henry Flood, an Irish-Protestant political leader, sponsored the Renunciation Act, which established Irish courts and extended the right of the Irish Parliament to write legislation.

THE UNITED IRISHMEN

These internal changes strengthened the movement for self-rule. In the late 1700s, Theobald Wolfe Tone, a Protestant lawyer from County Kildare, founded the Society of United Irishmen. Its purpose was to establish an independent Irish state in which Catholics and Protestants had the same rights. Tone left Ireland in 1795 because of pressure from both the British government and the Irish Parliament—which did not support the United Irishmen's cause. Tone sought military aid from France—the UK's rival—to mount a revolt.

In 1796 Tone sailed toward Ireland with 15,000 French troops, but stormy weather forced the fleet to return to France. Without foreign support, the Irish rebellion was easily put down by the British in 1798. The British captured Tone and sentenced him to death. Rather than die by hanging, Tone committed suicide.

Theobald Wolfe Tone led a combined group of Protestants and Catholics—the United Irishmen—in their fight against British authority in the late eighteenth century. He wanted to establish an independent Irish state in which all citizens—no matter what their religion—would have equal rights.

In order to resist the growing movement for an independent Ireland, the Irish Parliament passed the Act of Union in 1800. The act transferred Irish legislative power to the British Parliament. In 1801 Great Britain and Ireland were joined to form the United Kingdom of Great Britain and Ireland. The separate Irish legislature ceased to exist, and Ireland began sending representatives to the British Parliament.

Movements for Independence

With no parliament of their own, the Irish turned to strong local leaders who could influence the British government. One of these, the Irish lawyer Daniel O'Connell, used his skills as a public speaker and as a political organizer to remove limitations on Irish Catholics. Because of his efforts, Parliament passed the Catholic Emancipation Act, which allowed Catholics to be members of the British legislature. O'Connell next worked for the repeal of the Act of Union. He hoped that the Irish would once again have a separate assembly and be allowed to manage their own affairs.

Thousands of people attended open-air meetings to hear O'Connell speak in favor of greater self-rule. The popularity of the meetings prompted the British to stop the gatherings in 1843. They arrested O'Connell and sentenced him to prison for a year. His death in 1847 weakened the independence movement. Many Irish fled to the United States and France, where they organized resistance to British control of the island.

During this time, half of Ireland's eight million people lived in extreme poverty. Most of them depended on the annual potato crop for their staple food. In 1845 a blight (a disease caused by a fungus) destroyed that year's harvest of potatoes. Widespread famine occurred as the crops failed for the next several growing seasons. About one million Irish died from starvation or disease. Another million left the country, most going to North America. By

Courtesy of Library of Congress

Millions of Irish people left Ireland in the 1800s to start new lives in the United States. A drawing from the mid-nineteenth century shows the confusion and excitement of a group of Irish emigrants as they prepare to leave their country. By 1900 so many people had emigrated that the same number of Irish lived outside Ireland as within it.

1851 the population of Ireland had fallen to six million.

THE FENIAN BROTHERHOOD

Although it had weakened during the potato famine, the Irish independence movement had not died out completely. In 1858 John O'Mahoney, an Irish emigrant who lived in the United States, formed a secret society called the Fenian Brotherhood. The Fenians derived their name from a legendary group of warriors—called *fianna*—who had repelled invaders from the Irish coasts in about A.D. 200. The organization's purpose was to obtain Ireland's complete political independence from Britain. Another branch of the movement was located in Dublin and had much local support.

In March 1867, the Fenians led a revolt in Ireland. Although the British managed to put down the rebellion, they became more aware of their wrongs against the Irish. A new ally for Ireland appeared in the British prime minister, William Gladstone. He successfully sponsored legislation to end the favored status of Protestantism and to give Irish farmers more rights. Eventually the British government passed laws establishing fairer rents for Irish tenant farmers. New legislation also helped some Irish renters to purchase the land on which they worked.

CHARLES PARNELL AND HOME RULE

In 1875 Charles Stewart Parnell emerged as a leader from among the Protestants in Ireland, becoming a member of Parliament at the age of 29. Three years later he headed the Irish Nationalist party in the British Parliament. His main goal was a separate parliament for Ireland.

To the Irish people, Parnell was known simply as "the Chief"—a title that recalled

31

In the 1800s, British troops evicted and imprisoned many farmers who had stopped paying rent to their landlords. The farmers' defiant act, called a boycott, was part of a widespread movement to achieve land reform in Ireland.

ancient Irish leaders. He united two causes —land reform (the return of Irish land to Irish ownership) and home rule. Home rule meant that Ireland would control its internal affairs and that Britain would govern Ireland's trade, the military, and foreign policy. Parnell won the loyalty of a majority of Protestants and Catholics in Ireland.

Among Parnell's supporters was Michael Davitt, who was dedicated to improving conditions for Ireland's small-scale farmers. Parnell and Davitt combined their efforts in the Land League, which helped farmers to lower their rents and to gain ownership of the land they farmed. These two politicians encouraged tenant farmers to pay no rent at all—an action called a boycott—unless the landlords reduced the rent. (The word "boycott" comes from the name of Captain Charles Boycott, a land agent who refused to accept the lower rents that his farmers offered him.)

Some people carried these actions further than their leaders envisioned. Many Irish also boycotted anyone who gave any kind of service to boycotted landlords. The protests pressured Prime Minister Gladstone to sponsor another land-reform bill. The Land Act of 1881 reduced land rents by 20 percent and provided for another reduction in 15 years. These laws benefited many Irish farmers.

Sinn Fein

After Parnell's death in 1891, the movement for Irish rights slowed temporarily. In 1899 Arthur Griffith, a journalist, founded the *Sinn Fein* organization, whose name means "We Ourselves." Sinn Fein sponsored nonviolent resistance to British rule and urged Irish members of the British Parliament to withdraw from that legislative body.

Home rule continued to be a central issue. Those in favor of it—most Catholics and many Protestants—wanted independence, even if economic conditions worsened for a time. The people who opposed home rule—wealthy Irish Protestants and British people who had settled in northern Ireland—felt that their economic, social, and religious ties were with Britain. A home-rule law was passed in 1914. In that same year, however, Britain became involved in World War I, and home rule did not become a reality until the war ended.

During the war, about 160,000 Irish Volunteers enlisted in the British army. Members of Sinn Fein, however, were not satisfied with anything less than complete independence. Instead of joining the British war effort, about 12,000 of Sinn Fein's members formed the Irish Republican Brotherhood (IRB), a trained military force. The IRB and Sinn Fein planned a revolt that occurred on the Monday after Easter in 1916. On that day, about 1,000 rebel fighters seized the General Post Office and other buildings in Dublin, proclaiming the independence of the Irish Republic.

A large British force soon landed in Dublin to put down the rebellion. The British bombarded rebel-held buildings for four days. Most of the fighters surrendered, and 15 of the rebellion's leaders were executed. The executions strengthened public opinion on the side of Sinn Fein, whose candidates won a majority of the Irish seats in elections to the British Parliament in 1918.

Instead of attending the British Parliament, however, the Sinn Fein winners established their own legislature, or *Dail Eireann*, in Dublin in January 1919. The Dail claimed the right to make laws for all of Ireland and proclaimed the state of Ireland, or *Saorstat na hEireann*. Eamon De Valera, an IRB commander, helped to shape the Dail, and he was elected its president. Arthur Griffith, the founder of Sinn Fein, became vice-president.

Shortly after De Valera organized the Dail cabinet, violence erupted in Ireland again. David Lloyd George, Britain's prime minister, responded to the newly created Irish legislature by sending troops to Ireland. Among the troops was a special police force named the Black-and-Tans—so

In 1919 these Irishmen, although elected to the British Parliament, refused to take their seats and instead set up the first modern *Dail* (Irish legislature). Members in the front row include Michael Collins *(second from left)*, Arthur Griffith *(fourth from left)*, Eamon De Valera *(fifth from left)*, and William Cosgrave *(second from right)*.

Courtesy of Independent Newspapers, Dublin

In December 1921, Arthur Griffith *(left)* **and Michael Collins** *(right)* **walked in London during a break in negotiations with the British. The talks resulted in the birth of the Irish Free State.**

called because of the beige coats they wore over dark suits. These forces fiercely attacked the independence forces of the Sinn Fein, which had changed its name to the Irish Republican Army (IRA). The IRA engaged in guerrilla warfare and prompted a bitter response by the Black-and-Tans.

Finally, under Lloyd George's threat of immediate war in 1921, Arthur Griffith and Michael Collins (an IRA leader) signed a treaty that established the Irish Free State. This new, semi-independent nation had dominion status, meaning it retained some ties to Great Britain but was largely self-governing. An altered Home-Rule Bill of 1920 allowed the six counties of northeastern Ireland to remain part of the UK. This area, known as Ulster, strongly supported British rule.

Civil War

Some IRA members fiercely opposed the establishment of the Irish Free State. Instead, they wanted total independence from Great Britain. For 14 months, a civil war raged among Irish factions. During this time of fighting, the Irish independence movement lost two of its most prominent leaders. In August 1922, Arthur Griffith died of a stroke. In the same month, the IRA killed Michael Collins, who had run the temporary government

that was set up to carry out the treaty. A little-known figure—William Thomas Cosgrave—temporarily headed the government.

By 1926 Irish political leaders were divided into two factions. Some—known as conservatives—accepted the Irish Free State and believed in a gradual weakening of the bonds with Britain. The other group under De Valera's leadership disputed this course and wanted a fully independent state immediately. This group took the name *Fianna Fail*—meaning "warriors of destiny." Many of the Fianna Fail candidates were elected to the Dail. In 1932 Ireland held its most important general election under the Free State. De Valera's party won, defeating Cosgrave's government.

THE ESTABLISHMENT OF EIRE

In 1936, when a change of kings occurred in Britain, De Valera saw a chance to establish a new constitution. At the same time, he tried to set up a republic that included all of Ireland. The people of Ulster opposed becoming part of the larger Irish state. Nevertheless, in 1937 a new constitution was adopted for the residents of most of the island.

The Gaelic name for Ireland—Eire—replaced Irish Free State. Eire retained symbolic ties to the UK as a member of the British Commonwealth (association of states). De Valera became prime minister, and a Gaelic scholar and Protestant, Douglas Hyde, became president.

Eire's new status as an independent nation was tested when World War II broke out in 1939. The government quickly declared the country's neutrality in the conflict between Britain and Nazi Germany. Pressure from Great Britain and the United States—as well as air attacks by German planes—were not enough to convince the leaders of Eire to enter the war. Eire enforced strict censorship of news and would not allow information to circulate that might be regarded as unfriendly to any foreign power.

THE REPUBLIC OF IRELAND

In 1948 De Valera's Fianna Fail party did not win enough seats to remain in control of the Dail. John A. Costello—who arranged a coalition (combination) of several small Irish political parties—became prime minister. He demanded Ireland's complete independence from Great Britain. On April 18, 1949, Eire's elected Parliament officially declared the nation to be the Republic of Ireland. Ulster, or Northern Ireland, remained a separate country within the United Kingdom of Great Britain and Northern Ireland.

After the achievement of self-rule, Ireland continued to have severe economic problems. During the 1950s and 1960s, more than 25 percent of the working-age population were unemployed. Without jobs, half a million Irish people went to other nations to make a living. Only at the end of the 1950s did a new government administration begin seeking industrial expansion. In the 1960s, the tide of emigration slowed as new government programs created jobs.

As Ireland's economic outlook improved in the 1970s, the government turned to other pressing matters. Among them were its relations with Northern Ireland. An armed, anti-British segment of the Northern Ireland population had filled the ranks of the IRA. Most of the new members were Catholics who wanted to unite with the republic. Supported and supplied by IRA members in the south, the IRA in Northern Ireland fought for Irish unification.

In 1972 the republic took measures to control the IRA within the nation's borders. It also ended the special position

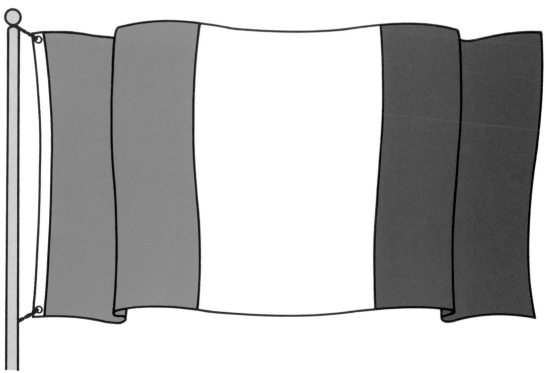

Artwork by Laura Westlund

First adopted in the mid-1800s, the three-color design of the Irish flag was modeled after the French national emblem. The order of the green, white, and orange bands was made official in 1937. Green represents the Roman Catholic population, and orange stands for the Protestant people of Ireland. The central white stripe symbolizes the hope for peace between the two groups.

given to the Roman Catholic Church by the Irish constitution. These measures were aimed at reducing the tensions between the republic and the predominantly Protestant population of Northern Ireland.

A further development reflecting the mood of the people of the republic came in early 1973. In that year, the dominant Fianna Fail party—long identified with the IRA—lost to a coalition of the Fine Gael and Socialist Labour parties. Liam Cosgrave, son of William Thomas Cosgrave, became prime minister.

Current Events

In 1974 the republic again tried to improve its relations with Northern Ireland. Liam Cosgrave declared that his government recognized Northern Ireland as a separate political division within the UK. The Irish government also announced its support

Courtesy of Government Information Services, Dublin, Ireland

Albert Reynolds was Ireland's prime minister from 1992 to 1994. He worked to reduce the country's unemployment rate and to stimulate the economy.

for British efforts to end IRA terrorism within the republic. The terrorism continued, however. In 1976 the British ambassador to Ireland, Christopher Ewart-Biggs, was killed when a land mine exploded beneath his car. Later that year, Ireland's legislature created the Emergency Powers Act, which gave the national government greater authority in combating terrorists.

In 1977 Fianna Fail won the general election, but the party's popularity soon faded. Irish voters were dissatisfied with a bad economy and unemployment rates of more than 20 percent. In the 1981 general election, Fianna Fail lost its majority. Since then frequently changing coalitions have governed Ireland.

In the same year, Britain and Ireland formed a council on Northern Ireland. Talks between the two countries resulted in the 1985 Anglo-Irish Agreement, which gave the Republic of Ireland the ability to advise the government of Northern Ireland without having any direct power. Despite Ireland's efforts, violence and political dissent persisted. By 1990 British, Irish, and Northern Irish officials were negotiating terms for discussions among all the parties involved in the Northern Ireland question. In late 1993, Irish prime minister Albert Reynolds and British prime minister John Major issued the Downing Street Declaration. The declaration set out guidelines for peace talks and specified that Northern Irish voters had to approve any action taken.

In addition to political problems, economic difficulties weighed on Ireland. But in the early 1990s, the country's economy began to rebound. In 1992 Irish voters approved the Maastricht treaty, which provided closer economic and political ties for the nations of the European Union (EU). When the treaty was passed that year, Ireland became eligible for billions of dollars in aid. In 1993 lawmakers created a job fund and increased spending on health and education.

The dome of the Four Courts, which houses Ireland's highest judicial bodies, rises above the Liffey River. Originally constructed in the 1700s, this governmental building was reduced to a shell at the beginning of the Irish civil war in 1921 but had been restored by 1932.

Ireland's economic recovery became a boom in the mid-1990s. The country stands poised to enter the next century with one of the fastest-growing economies in the EU.

Government

The lawmaking body of Ireland is Parliament, which consists of the president of Ireland and two houses—the Assembly (*Dail Eireann*, known as the Dail) and the Senate (*Seanad Eireann*). Voters elect the 166 members of the Dail. The Senate is composed of 60 delegates, 11 of whom are nominated by the prime minister and 49 of whom are elected. The University of Dublin, the National University of Ireland, and five panels of professional, trade, and cultural associations elect the senators.

Citizens who are 18 years of age and older directly elect the president of Ireland. This executive leader holds office for seven years and is eligible for reelection only once. The president appoints a prime minister, who is the leader of the majority party in the Dail. The prime minister then appoints a cabinet of ministers who must be approved by the Dail. A seven-member Council of State—which includes chief justices, legislative delegates, and former prime ministers—advises the president.

The president appoints judges to the courts of Ireland. The highest court is the supreme court, which is made up of five judges. It handles the most difficult legal questions and determines the constitutionality of laws passed by the Irish legislature. A court of criminal appeals handles criminal cases that need review. A high court deals with both civil and criminal cases. Circuit and district courts decide minor legal questions.

Ireland is divided into 26 counties, and much of the administration of the country is carried on through county boards. Membership in these bodies is by popular election for terms of five years. The national department of local government coordinates the actions of all of the county boards.

These children live in the village of Louisburgh in western Ireland. About 25 percent of Ireland's 3.6 million people are under the age of 15.

3) The People

Within its small land area, Ireland has an evenly distributed population of 3.6 million people. One major division occurs between the Irish who live on either side of the Shannon River. Those on the eastern side generally are part of a more industrial society and have a higher standard of living. East of the Shannon, farmland is usually more productive.

People on the western side of the Shannon River live in a less fertile farming area, have fewer industrial areas, and inhabit smaller population centers. Along the western seaboard lies the *Gaeltacht*—a region where many people speak Gaelic as their everyday language. The people of the Gaeltacht still follow a number of Irish traditions in their daily lives.

Ethnic Identity and Language

Most Irish people trace their ancestry to the Celts, Vikings, Normans, and English who arrived in Ireland during the last 2,000 years. These immigrants and conquerors intermarried with one another and

Many older houses in rural areas of Ireland have thatched roofs and stone walls. Irish people often plant flowers in their yards and maintain small vegetable gardens.

with the descendants of the earliest inhabitants of the island. In recent years, a small number of immigrants have adopted Ireland as their home. Among them are Eastern Europeans, Italians, East Indians, Chinese, and Vietnamese.

The Irish government strengthens Irish identity and culture by encouraging the use of Gaelic. The people of Ireland spoke Gaelic until about 1200, when the Norman-English took control of much of the country. Over the years, Norman-English

soldiers, traders, artists, farmers, and political leaders introduced the English language to the residents of the island. By the 1850s, the use of English was dominant in every region of Ireland except the far west. A movement to preserve Gaelic spread as part of the drive for nationhood that began at the end of the nineteenth century.

Currently, about one Irish person in four can speak some Gaelic. Many more can understand it when it is spoken by others. The constitution names Gaelic as the

Originally owned by a Norman-English family whose soldiers conquered the area, Ashford Castle stands near Cong in western Ireland. Enlarged in the eighteenth century, the castle is now a hotel.

nation's first language, with English as the second official tongue. Street signs and government documents are printed in both languages. All schools—especially in areas where the language has fallen into disuse —teach Gaelic. Spoken most frequently along the western coast, Gaelic is often heard in radio and television broadcasts.

Religion

Since 1973 the Irish constitution has guaranteed freedom of religion. Although 95 percent of the population are Roman Catholic, the nation has no official state religion. Most of the remaining 5 percent of the people belong to either the Church of Ireland (Episcopalian), the Methodist Church, the Presbyterian Church, or the Jewish faith.

Membership in the Roman Catholic Church provides a strong common bond for most Irish people. Teachings from this faith have influenced Irish legislators as they enact laws—particularly those concerning family life, divorce, and abortion. Roman Catholicism has also played a significant part in the development of Irish culture.

Persecution by British rulers who tried to extinguish Roman Catholicism only caused most Irish Catholics to cling to their religion. Catholic practices dominate much of daily life. The religion has influenced architecture, education, and local festivals. Many Irish people belong to social organizations connected to the Church, and they participate in a wide range of cultural events sponsored by their local religious community.

Photo by Kay Shaw Photography

Signs in Ireland are often printed in both Gaelic and English, the country's two official languages. This sign indicates where the women's restroom is in a train station. Only a small percentage of the nation's people speak Gaelic on a daily basis, but everyone learns the basics of the language in school.

Dating from the tenth century, Muiredach's Cross in eastern Ireland stands more than 16 feet tall. Carved with biblical scenes on all four sides, this sandstone cross is one of the largest such memorials in Ireland.

The interior of St. Patrick's Cathedral in Dublin shows the skill of Christian architects and workers who carefully crafted the structure. The Gothic style of tall windows and pointed arches creates a quiet religious atmosphere.

Danish Vikings laid the foundation of Christ Church Cathedral in Dublin in the eleventh century. The building was reconstructed in the late 1800s and still contains the crypt (underground burial area) from the earlier era.

This public house (pub) in Dingle is typical of Irish gathering places, where people come to find refreshments, food, and conversation.

A young Irish boy carries bricks of dried peat from the family's storage shed into the house. Many Irish burn peat in their fireplaces instead of wood.

Way of Life

Although 56 percent of the Irish live in urban areas, most of these people reside in medium-sized towns rather than in large metropolitan areas. Many of Ireland's farm families live in small villages close to their fields. Some rural people still dwell in nineteenth-century Irish houses, which have stone or brick walls and thatched roofs. One common method of heating rural homes—as well as residences in some urban areas—is by burning dried peat.

Communities of all sizes have "pubs"— an abbreviation for public houses. At these places, residents of a neighborhood often go to visit with one another, to share refreshments, and sometimes to have a meal. Earlier in the twentieth century, many pubs served a largely male clientele, but in recent decades women have become regular patrons as well.

Women in Ireland have broadened the range of roles that they play in society. In the past, most married women raised a family and managed a home. Those who lived in rural areas took on a large share of the farm work. After achieving higher educational levels in the 1970s and 1980s, more women are participating in business, government, and professional life. Advancement for women in these areas is often hindered by Irish people who prefer that women play a traditional role.

Education, Health, and Welfare

About 99 percent of the people in Ireland can read and write. School is compulsory for children between the ages of 6 and 15. Private organizations—usually local Catholic or Episcopalian churches—administer most schools, while the government provides financial support and oversees curriculum development. Most schools have either all boys or all girls as students.

Secondary schools focus either on general or vocational education.

The oldest school of higher learning in Ireland is Trinity College, which was founded in 1591. Also known as the University of Dublin, this school has about 8,000 students. The National University of Ireland—established in 1909—has its main branch in Dublin and has other campuses in Cork and Galway. Located in Maynooth, St. Patrick's College began in 1795. It houses the national seminary for training Roman Catholic priests and is associated with the National University.

The Irish government has organized a health system that is based on a person's ability to pay for services. In addition, Irish workers, their employers, and the government support a system of social welfare. Its programs provide funds to widows, orphaned children, retired people,

More than 90 percent of the schools in Ireland are operated by the Roman Catholic Church—the religious organization to which most Irish belong. These girls attend a government-funded elementary school in County Galway, and Roman Catholic nuns run the school. Classes are taught in Gaelic, but students may take English as one of their subjects. History, mathematics, science, health, and geography are also studied at this level.

Courtesy of Tom Moran

Independent Picture Service

This fisherman and his daughter live on one of the three Aran Islands. Lying in the Atlantic Ocean about 25 miles from Galway City, the islands are known for the production of fine woolen yarn, which Aran knitters make into beautiful clothing.

disabled citizens, unwed mothers, and unemployed laborers.

Low-income citizens get most of their medical care free of charge. Children throughout Ireland receive free hospital care until the age of 16. The country's health boards furnish medications for people who suffer from long-term health problems or from infectious diseases. Ireland's health statistics compare well with those of the rest of Europe. In Ireland about 5.9 babies out of 1,000 die before they reach the age of 1, while the average for Europe is 11 per 1,000. Life expectancy in Ireland is 76 years, higher than the average figure of 73 for all of Europe.

Literature and Drama

After they conquered Ireland around 250 B.C., the Celts developed a rich literary

Photo by Michelle Hannah

Trinity College enrolls about 8,000 students. Its graduates include the writers Jonathan Swift, Oliver Goldsmith, J. M. Synge, Oscar Wilde, and Samuel Beckett. Colleges in Ireland have a combined attendance of more than 30,000 people. The Irish government also funds technical schools that are located in many parts of the country.

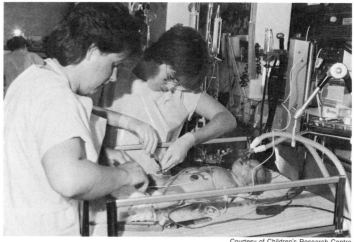

Courtesy of Children's Research Centre

tradition on the island. Historians collected the age-old stories, and poets memorized these tales by transforming them into complex rhymes.

Many writers of later periods took their inspiration from local problems and from everyday life. In general, these authors wrote in English, rather than in Gaelic.

Jonathan Swift was born in Dublin during the late seventeenth century. After studying at Trinity College, he became a minister in the Church of Ireland. He wrote many of his works with the intention of informing the general public—especially British politicians—of injustices within Ireland. *Gulliver's Travels*, his most

William Butler Yeats was born in Dublin in 1865. His early poetry told the story of Ireland's past heroes. He also wrote plays that were produced at the Abbey Theatre, the playhouse he and his associates founded in Dublin. Yeats wrote the poem *Easter 1916* in honor of those who died in the uprising that led to Ireland's independence.

Courtesy of Irish Tourist Board, New York

Jonathan Swift penned *Gulliver's Travels* both as a funny children's story and as a social commentary for adults on unjust conditions in Ireland. This painting illustrates a scene from the novel. After Gulliver has collapsed on a beach, he wakes to find himself tied to the ground and surrounded by tiny people called Lilliputians.

famous work, tells of four voyages to make-believe lands. Through his accounts of the people in these strange places, Swift poked fun at human behavior.

Born in Ireland in 1730, Oliver Goldsmith turned to writing after failing to make a living as a doctor. The author of many novels and plays, he drew upon experiences of his native Ireland to write two of his most famous works, *The Vicar of Wakefield* and *She Stoops to Conquer*.

Ireland has produced many modern writers who were influenced by the early historians and poets. James Joyce was one who in turn influenced twentieth-century authors through his technique of stream-of-consciousness writing, in which he portrayed his characters' thoughts in sequence and great detail. His major works include *Portrait of the Artist as a Young Man, Ulysses,* and *Finnegan's Wake.* William Butler Yeats, who lived at the same time as Joyce, was one of the country's leading playwrights and poets. In 1923 Yeats received the Nobel Prize for literature.

J. M. Synge chronicled Irish rural life in his plays *Riders to the Sea* and *Playboy of the Western World.* George Bernard Shaw, who was born in Ireland but spent most of his life in Britain, wrote plays that made fun of English society and that revealed serious social problems. In *Juno and the Paycock* and *The Plough and the Stars,* the dramatist Sean O'Casey explored the upheaval of the Irish civil war. Samuel Beckett, another influence on modern drama, won a Nobel Prize for literature in 1969. One of his most famous plays is *Waiting for Godot.* J. B. Keane and Maeve Binchy are among the many talented contemporary writers in Ireland.

Art, Music, and Handicrafts

Ireland has produced many artists since the nineteenth century. John Keating and Estella Solomon painted scenes of the rural landscape of their country. Mainie Jellett, Jack B. Yeats, and Tony O'Malley, among others, created works in a more modern, abstract style. Since 1951 the Arts Council, which the government funds, has supported the work of many artists in Ireland.

The tradition of Irish folk music is rich and thriving. Schools and churches provide opportunities for young people to learn to play age-old instruments, including the Celtic harp, the flute, bagpipes, the

Bagpipes (wind instruments) are used by musicians who play traditional Irish music.

At the Abbey Theatre, Irish actors pose together after a performance of J. M. Synge's *Playboy of the Western World*.

A musician plays a Celtic harp during a re-creation of medieval life at one of Ireland's castles.

47

The popular musical group U2 performs throughout the world. In their recordings and concerts, these Irish musicians include songs about human rights and social justice.

Photo by Anton Corbijn

bodhran (a hand-held drum), and the accordion. Many pubs are gathering places for informal musical performances. At religious gatherings and town or regional festivals, musicians play jigs, reels, and other centuries-old tunes. Traditional Irish dancing often accompanies folk music.

The Chieftains are a well-known professional group that plays in the traditional style. The contemporary Irish rock group U2—which identifies social problems through its lyrics—also plays to audiences worldwide. Bob Geldof, an Irish singer, organized a worldwide fundraising benefit in 1985 to help ease hunger in Africa.

For centuries, the Irish have shown extraordinary skill and artistry in making handicrafts, especially in weaving linen and tweed and in making Waterford crystal glass. The oldest candle-making firm in Europe, Rathborne, has been producing candles for more than 450 years. Belleek china is treasured for its purity of design and its quality.

Photo by Irish Tourist Board, Dublin

A symphony orchestra plays for an audience at the National Concert Hall in Dublin. The capital city provides opportunities to hear fine classical music as well as Irish folk music.

One of Ireland's master glassblowers creates a pitcher. After molding hot glass into the desired shape, he removes the excess before adding the handle and spout.

Continually turning his potter's wheel, an Irish artisan forms wet clay into a large bowl. Irish crafts, such as pottery and glass, are made by hand, and their sale—mainly to tourists—adds to the Irish economy.

Sports

Ireland has many sports enthusiasts. They enjoy participating in or watching horse racing, golfing, fishing, hunting, Gaelic football, hurling (a kind of field hockey), soccer, rugby, and greyhound dog racing. Irish racehorses have earned a reputation as outstanding competitors at home and abroad. Horse racing is one of the most popular of Irish sports, and the Irish pay particular attention to the Irish Derby and other annual races. Jumping competitions at the Dublin Horse Show attract thousands of people each August.

Golf is another popular sport in Ireland, with over 200 courses kept in playing condition year-round. Various championships, including the Irish Hospitals' 72-hole tournament, attract large crowds. Ireland's lakes, streams, and rivers provide more

Courtesy of Irish Tourist Board, New York

Near an ancient castle, a fisherman tries his skill in southeastern Ireland's Nore River.

This golf course lies near the Irish Sea, close to the mouth of the Shannon River. The winds from the water and the challenging layout of the course make these links popular with both professional and amateur golfers.

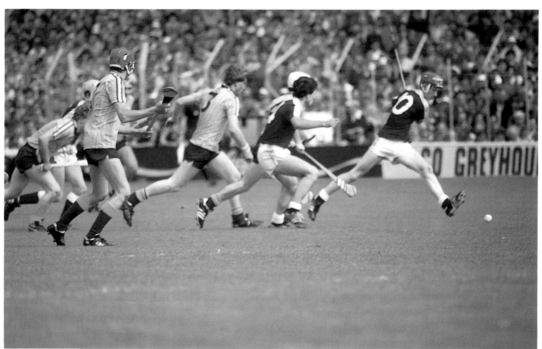

The members of hurling teams use three-foot-long sticks (called hurleys) that have curved ends. With these sticks, the athletes try to move a small leather-covered ball through their opponents' goalposts.

than 900 square miles of fresh water that abound with fish—including salmon, brown trout, pike, and perch. Coastal fishing yields salmon, sea trout, sea bass, and blue shark. The Irish are also fond of hunting and target shooting.

Food

Many Irish meals feature boiled potatoes, onions, herbs, and some kind of meat. This combination made with mutton (the meat of sheep) is called Irish stew. Cabbage, potatoes, onions, and herbs are the ingredients of a dish named colcannon. Beef, chicken, pork, veal, lamb, and mutton frequently appear in Irish cooking. Many

people in rural Ireland grown their own potatoes and use them in their daily meals.

Along the coasts, people enjoy fresh lobsters, prawns, oysters, and other seafoods. Plaice and trout are also popular with many Irish people. Soda bread, with its hard outer crust and soft interior, is served with most meals. Scones, tarts, special breads, and cakes may accompany tea at the end of meals.

In homes and at pubs, the alcoholic beverage most often served to adults is a stout beer. This drink is usually referred to by the name of the largest Irish company—Guinness—that produces it. Irish whiskey is sold around the world as well as in its land of origin.

Rugby is a fast-moving game with exciting runs and rough tackles. The 15 players on each side try to score points by carrying an oblong, inflated ball across the other team's goal line. These participants from Trinity College find themselves engaged in a very muddy match.

Courtesy of Colleen Riley

A cook demonstrates how to make soda bread, whose ingredients include baking soda, flour, and buttermilk. The bread is often part of a traditional Irish breakfast.

Photo by Kay Shaw Photography

The shipyard at Cork serves as a repair and maintenance dock for vessels from Ireland and other European countries.

4) The Economy

Lacking many natural resources, Ireland had a difficult time in the first half of the twentieth century adjusting its economy to modern industry. In the 1950s and 1960s, the Irish government began programs that encouraged investors to build industrial centers. Since then, Irish economic planners have continued to seek ways to bring Irish goods into world markets and to speed national development.

In 1973 Ireland became a member of the European Union (EU)—an association of western European nations dedicated to improving economic conditions among themselves. As a result of this move, Ireland's trade with the rest of Europe has improved. The EU plans to remove all commercial barriers among its members, forming a powerful trading group.

Magee's factory in Donegal Town makes woolen fabric, including tweed. An important national export, the tweed of western Ireland is famous for its beauty and strength.

Manufacturing and Trade

The government started to help Irish industries grow in the late 1950s. New jobs in manufacturing plants enabled more Irish workers to make a living in their homeland. By 1974 emigration had tapered off as more industrial jobs became available. By 1978 some Irish emigrants were returning. In 1990 almost 30 percent of Irish workers were employed in the nation's manufacturing industries.

The government has encouraged both Irish and foreign firms to build new manufacturing plants by offering grants and tax benefits. Ireland's highly educated work force has attracted investors from North America, Europe, and Japan. Their factories produce electrical components, car parts, pharmaceuticals, and other goods. During the 1990s, these plants helped Ireland's economy to grow at one of the fastest rates in the EU.

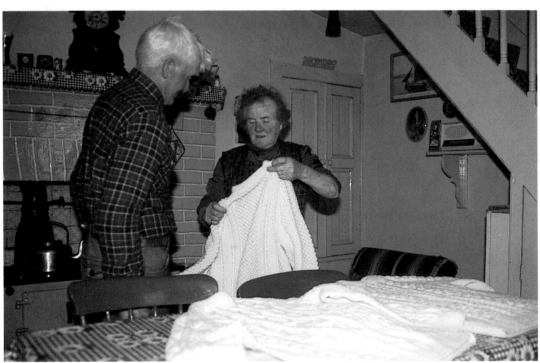

At her home on one of the Aran Islands, a knitter shows her work to a customer. The high quality of the yarn and the intricate patterns in the clothing make Aran sweaters popular throughout the world.

A craftsman from a glass factory near Galway completes the detailed grinding on a piece of decorative Galway crystal.

The Irish have exported woolen and linen goods abroad for several centuries. Knitters from the Aran Islands make sweaters with distinctive designs that are popular throughout the world. Consumers also prize fine Irish glassware. Ireland's largest industries package meat, grain, and dairy products. More recent manufactured exports include beer, shoes, glassware, electrical parts, computer components, and machinery.

In the 1940s, the Irish government imposed tariffs (import taxes) on foreign goods to discourage other nations from selling their products in Ireland. The government's measures were meant to help Irish industries survive. But these same laws made Ireland an unattractive place for foreign businesses.

When Ireland lowered most of its tariffs in the 1950s, other countries responded by lowering their own tariffs on Irish goods. Trade increased, and businesses from other nations began to seek investment opportunities in Ireland. These trends continued to improve Ireland's economic outlook in the 1990s.

About 30 percent of Ireland's trade occurs with Great Britain and Northern Ireland. As a member of the EU, Ireland has been able to take advantage of increased trade opportunities with countries on the continent and to receive economic assistance from the EU.

Agriculture and Fishing

Although manufacturing has become Ireland's primary economic activity, agriculture still brings in 9 percent of the national income and employs 13 percent of the work force. Some people operate small subsistence farms on which farmers raise only enough to feed their families. Others run highly mechanized commercial farms that produce grain, milk, and meat for export.

Farmland covers about 70 percent of Ireland, and 85 percent of this fertile soil is pastureland. The government provides fertilizers that improve the grasslands on which beef and dairy cattle graze. Beef—the main farm product—accounts for 60 percent of Ireland's agricultural exports, with dairy products providing another 12 percent. With better grass and improved breeds of cows, milk production has the potential to offer the farmer more income than beef production has. Other Irish agricultural items include potatoes, barley, sugar beets, wheat, sheep, and hogs. Irish farmers and horse breeders also raise many fine purebred horses.

Although Ireland's inland streams and lakes have been fished successfully for many years, the nation's deep-sea waters have produced large catches only since the 1980s. Many of Ireland's farmers and sport fishermen take salmon, eel, and trout from the country's rivers and lakes, Increasing numbers of commercial boats haul mackerel, cod, herring, lobster, and shrimp from the oceans and seas surrounding Ireland.

Photo by Kay Shaw Photography

In southwestern Ireland, a worker shears a sheep's thick wool, which can be spun into yarn.

Photo by Irish Tourist Board, Dublin

Tourists can hire a boat to test their skill at deep-sea fishing. Professional fishermen ply Ireland's coastal waters daily in search of mackerel, cod, and shrimp.

Photo by Kay Shaw Photography

A farmer operates a hay-cutting machine pulled by a horse. Many of Ireland's small farms use horse-drawn machinery.

Independent Picture Service

Members of an Irish family work together in their potato field. Although no longer a leading crop, potatoes are still an important part of the nation's agricultural output.

57

Tourism and Transportation

About 3.5 million people visit Ireland each year. More than half of the tourists who come to Ireland are from Great Britain. Many are from the United States, whose population was increased by large-scale immigration from Ireland in the 1800s and 1900s. As a result of this history, many visitors from the United States come to Ireland to find out about their family roots. Others are attracted by the country's natural beauty and its historical sites. Travelers often attend cultural events, such as musical performances, horse races, and theatrical plays.

Tourists support the service industry, whose workers sell food and drink, provide accommodations, and work in retail shops.

Visitors also create a greater need for government workers such as police and customs officials. The entire service industry in Ireland—including tourism—is responsible for about 55 percent of the national earnings.

Most travelers arrive in Ireland by air at Shannon, Dublin, or Cork—the nation's three international airports. Aer Lingus is Ireland's national airline and handles a large share of traffic to and from the country. About 60,000 miles of roads connect Ireland's cities and towns. The nation's bus system reaches every population center on the island. A state-owned railway system also serves all the main population centers and links many smaller towns as well.

Courtesy of Irish Tourist Board, New York

A group of horseback riders follows the seashore on its way through the countryside. Ireland's beautiful scenery, historic sites, and friendly people draw millions of visitors each year. Many people who come to the republic from other countries are of Irish ancestry.

A group of young tourists weathers a gentle shower in a Dublin garden. Travelers to Ireland are usually advised to bring adequate rain gear.

Dublin Airport handles a large flow of international air traffic. Aer Lingus is the national airline, and its planes sport a shamrock on their tails as a company emblem.

A huge pile of dried, machine-harvested peat fuels this power plant in central Ireland. The facility's large cooling tower brings the high temperature of the water used in generating electricity back to a normal level.

Almost all of Ireland's international shipping—which carries a considerable portion of the trade between Ireland and other European countries—goes through Dublin, Cork, or Waterford. Ports in smaller towns are important for water transport along the coast. There are several cross-channel services between Great Britain and Ireland. Ferry services have regular routes between Dublin and Holyhead in Wales and between Dublin and Liverpool in England. Boats also travel from Rosslare in Ireland to Pembroke in Wales.

Mining and Energy

In 1970 Irish miners discovered some of Europe's largest supplies of lead and zinc in eastern Ireland. The nation exports a large percentage of these newfound metal resources to Europe. Coal, on the other hand, is in short supply, and almost all the nation's supply must be imported.

Dried peat heats many of Ireland's homes and provides about 18 percent of

In western Ireland, a ferry takes passengers and their vehicles across a narrow section of the Shannon River between Killimer and Tarbert. The trip saves travelers from having to drive the 55 miles around the waterway.

the republic's energy. People cut peat from the ground in small blocks and then stack it on end to dry it out. When the blocks are dry enough to be burned, they are taken to people's homes. Machines harvest the much larger amounts of peat that are used in some of the country's electricity generating plants.

Imported petroleum fills about 50 percent of Ireland's energy needs. Engineers discovered natural gas off Ireland's southern coast, and in the mid-1980s wells began to bring the gas to the surface. Petroleum has been found off the southern and eastern coasts of the country. Britain and Ireland are negotiating to build a pipeline across the Irish Sea. The pipeline will transport oil and natural gas to Ireland from the North Sea, where Britain's energy deposits lie.

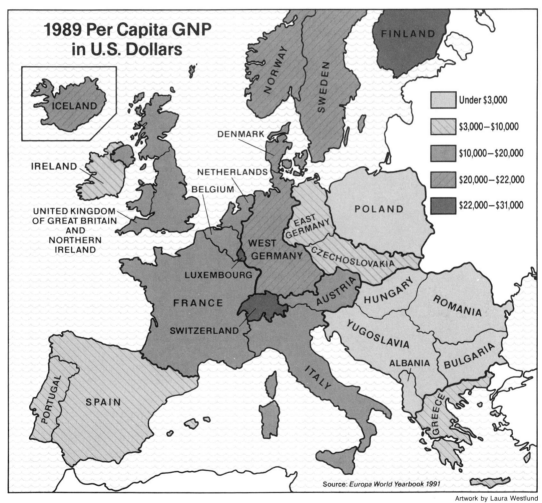

This map compares the average wealth per person—calculated by gross national product (GNP) per capita—for 26 European countries. The GNP is the value of all goods and services produced by a country in a year. To arrive at the GNP per capita, each nation's total GNP is divided by its population figure. The resulting dollar amounts indicate one measure of the standard of living in each country. Ireland's 1994 figure of $13,630, up from $9,550 in 1989, reflects an improving economy but still puts the country among Europe's poorer nations.

A farmer hauls peat to burn in his fireplace. Peat forms over a long period of time when decayed vegetation becomes packed down in swamps or marshes. After cutting the peat by hand and drying it in the sun, many rural Irish use it as a low-cost fuel.

Photo by Irish Tourist Board, Dublin

People line the streets in Dublin to watch a parade on St. Patrick's Day (March 17). An actor dressed as Charlie Chaplin's the Tramp—a comic character from the early days of movies—entertains young and old alike.

The Future

Although Ireland has already addressed some modern economic problems, Irish planners face serious challenges in the new century. With the continuing development of the EU, Ireland will have more opportunities to sell its goods on the continent. At the same time, however, Irish products will encounter stiff competition from other European countries. More than ever, Ireland needs to give its young workers reasons to remain in Ireland.

Solving the difficulties in Northern Ireland is also important to the future of Ireland. Britain and Ireland continue to work together in search of ways to end the violence that has claimed many lives.

Despite its economic and social problems, Ireland remains a nation dominated by green fields and small towns. Ireland's challenges include sustaining economic growth and higher employment among its people. These goals stand alongside the desire to maintain the benefits of an unhurried rural existence within an increasingly urbanized world.

Photo by Irish Tourist Board, Dublin

Hikers make their way along a stretch of Ireland's rocky, green countryside, which continues to charm and challenge visitors. The Irish also have a great fondness for their homeland, as it offers an improved quality of life for its citizens.

Index